Carol Stream Public Library
616 Hiawatha Drive
Carol Stream, Illinois 60188

MEASURING

AT THE DOG SHOW

by Amy Rauen

Illustrations by Lorin Walter

Reading consultant: Susan Nations, M.Ed., author/
literacy coach/consultant in literacy development

Math consultant: Rhea Stewart, M.A., mathematics content specialist

WEEKLY READER®

PUBLISHING

Dog
Show

There is a dog show today. I will go
with Mom. Mom knows I love dogs.

4

There are many dogs here. Some are longer than others. Some are shorter than others.

I want to find the longest dog at the
dog show. We see some long dogs.
Mom will help me measure them.

We need to use something to measure
the dogs. Can we use our hands?

Mom says our hands are not the same length. Her hands are longer than mine. We need to measure with objects that are the same length.

We see cans of dog food. Each can
is the same length. Mom asks if we can
use them. We will measure the dogs
with cans. We lay the cans end-to-end.

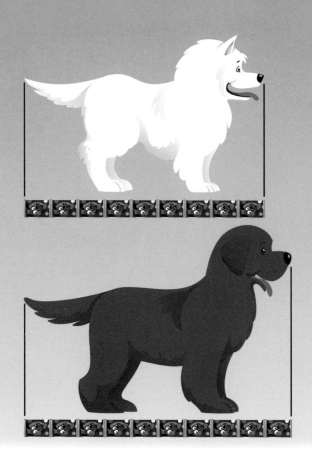

We measure the dogs from nose to tail. Look, the white dog is 9 cans long. The brown dog is 10 cans long. The brown dog is longer than the white dog.

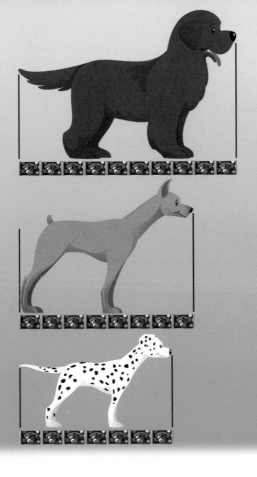

Mom and I measure two more dogs. The tan dog is 8 cans long. The spotted dog is 7 cans long. The brown dog is longer than each of these dogs.

Mom and I measure many dogs. The brown dog is still the longest. There are two dogs left. One has long, white fur. The other dog is gray.

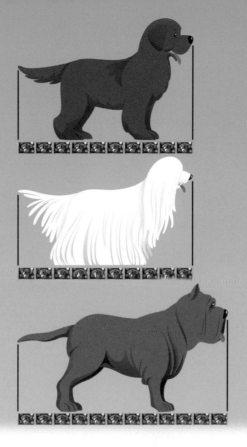

The white dog is 10 cans long. It is the same length as the brown dog. The gray dog is 12 cans long. It is longer than the brown dog. The gray dog is the longest dog at the dog show!

I want to find the shortest dog at the dog show. We see some small dogs. Mom will help me measure them.

We need to use something to measure
the small dogs. We see some dog combs.
Mom asks if we can use them to measure
the dogs.

We see three dogs. Mom and I lay
the combs end-to-end. We measure
each dog from nose to tail.

The white dog is 5 combs long. The black dog is 6 combs long. The gray dog is 4 combs long. The gray dog is the shortest dog we have found.

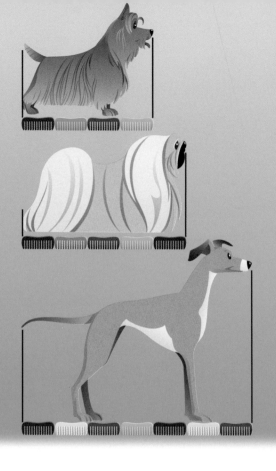

Mom and I measure two more dogs.
The long-haired dog is 5 combs long.
The short-haired dog is 7 combs long.
The gray dog is still the shortest dog.

Mom and I measure more dogs. The gray dog is the shortest dog so far. There are four dogs left to measure.

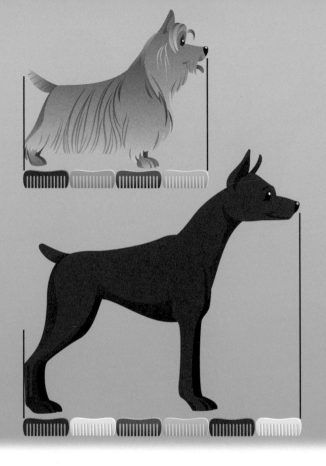

The brown dog is 6 combs long.
The gray dog is still shorter.

The black dog is 4 combs long. It is
the same length as the gray dog.

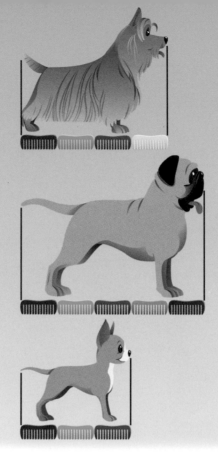

The dog with black ears is 5 combs long. The gray dog is shorter than this dog. The tan dog is only 3 combs long. It is shorter than the gray dog.

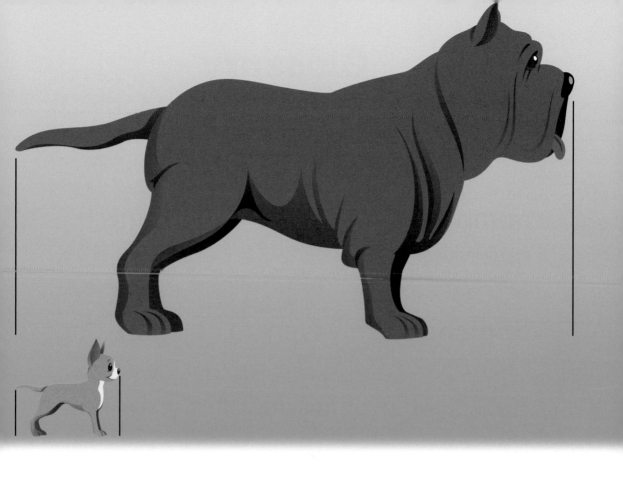

The tan dog is the shortest dog at the
dog show. The gray dog is the longest
dog. Mom and I found the longest dog
and the shortest dog!

23

Glossary

can – a container for holding food or other objects

comb – a tool used to arrange hair or fur

dog show – an event to compare dogs

fur – the soft, hairy coat of an animal

About the Author

Amy Rauen is the author of thirteen math books for children. She also designs and writes educational software. Amy lives in San Diego, California, with her husband and their two cats.

Please visit our web site at: www.garethstevens.com
For a free color catalog describing our list of high-quality books,
call 1-800-542-2595 (USA) or 1-800-387-3178 (Canada).

Library of Congress Cataloging-in-Publication Data

Rauen, Amy.
    Measuring at the dog show / Amy Rauen — North American ed.
      p. cm. — (Math in our world)
    ISBN-13: 978-0-8368-8474-6 (lib. bdg.)
    ISBN-10: 0-8368-8474-4 (lib. bdg.)
    ISBN-13: 978-0-8368-8483-8 (softcover)
    ISBN-10: 0-8368-8483-3 (softcover)
    1. Length measurement—Juvenile literature. 2. Dog shows—
Juvenile literature. I. Title.
    QC102.R38   2007
    516'.15—dc22
                               2007017945

This edition first published in 2008 by
Weekly Reader® Books
An imprint of Gareth Stevens Publishing
1 Reader's Digest Road
Pleasantville, NY 10570-7000 USA

Copyright © 2008 by Gareth Stevens, Inc.

Managing editor: Dorothy L. Gibbs
Art direction: Tammy West
Illustrations: Lorin Walter

Printed in the United States of America

1 2 3 4 5 6 7 8 9 11 10 09 08 07

MEASURING

AT THE DOG SHOW